Illustrated by Mike Higgs

Written by Sally McNulty

ISBN 0 00 197141 7

Printed in Italy

Collins

London and Glasgow

Mark's new telescope was his best birthday present. One night he was looking through it at the moon. "I wish I knew more about the moon," he said out loud.

"I was flying past and heard what you said," announced Moonbird flying in through an open window. "I know a lot of things about the moon. I will be happy to tell you about the moon."

"No one is really sure where the moon came from," said Moonbird. "Some people think the moon broke off from the earth billions of years ago. Others think it may have come from another part of space and stayed to circle around the earth.

"The Moon was formed about 4 billion years ago. At that time the whole moon was so hot, it was like the inside of a volcano. It was a mass of melted rocks. The outer crust slowly cooled and turned hard."

THE MOON IS A SATELLITE. IT CIRCLES AROUND EARTH.

THE MOON EITHER SPLIT FROM THE EARTH OR CAME FROM ANOTHER PART OF SPACE AND STAYED TO CIRCLE THE EARTH.
HOT CENTRE
CRUST
A SATELLITE IS A SMALLER WORLD THAT CIRCLES AROUND A LARGER WORLD.

"While the crust was still warm, giant rocks called meteorites crashed into the moon. The meteorites made flat holes many miles wide called craters. Some craters have walls two miles high. Next molten lava rushed up from inside the moon into deep cracks in the moon's surface. When the lava cooled it formed large, smooth places. We call them seas," Moonbird continued.

A METEORITE IS A METAL OR MINERAL MASS THAT HAS FALLEN ONTO THE MOON FROM OUTER SPACE.

MOLTEN LAVA IS HOT MELTED ROCKS.

“They are not real seas because there is no water on the moon. They just look like seas from the earth. The moon looks like a big, round, shiny ball,” said Moonbird. “It has dark parts and light parts. Sometimes we think we can see a face in the moon.”

A SEA ON THE MOON IS NOT A REAL SEA. IT IS A LARGE, FLAT PLACE.

DARK PARTS OF THE MOON LOOK LIKE EYES, NOSE AND MOUTH. WE THINK WE SEE A “MAN IN THE MOON”.

"The moon has no light of its own," Moonbird told Mark. "What we call moonlight is really the sun's light shining on the moon. The sun lights up earth too. Earth looks bright when seen from the moon. The moon is closer to the sun than earth is. Wherever sun shines on the moon, the moon gets very hot. It is too hot for people to live there. Astronauts need specially cooled space suits to go there."

WHERE SUN SHINES ON THE MOON IT CAN BE 265 DEGREES F.

“One day on the moon lasts two weeks. One night last two weeks. At night it is so cold a person would quickly freeze. You would need heat in your space suit to keep warm. I will take you on a secret trip to the moon in a magic bubble,” Moonbird told Mark.

"You must not tell anyone," said Moonbird. Mark promised not to tell. "If a car drove 65 miles an hour without stopping," Moonbird said, "it would take five months for the car to reach the moon. A spaceship with rockets can reach the moon in three days."

THE MOON IS ABOUT 240 THOUSAND MILES FROM THE EARTH.

“Sometimes the moon looks round. Other times it looks thin,” said Mark.

“The moon never changes its shape,” said Moonbird. “As the moon circles the earth, you can only see the part that is lit up by the sun.”

"It takes the moon about 28 days to go completely around the earth. Sometimes you can see a lot of the moon. Sometimes you can only see a little. Sometimes you do not see the moon at all."

THE PATH TAKEN BY THE MOON AS IT CIRCLES THE EARTH IS CALLED AN "ORBIT".

"You cannot see the moon when the moon is between the earth and the sun," Moonbird explained. "At that time the sun is lighting up the far side of the moon and the side facing earth is in darkness."

"The same side of the moon always faces earth. It is called the 'near side'. The 'far side' of the moon always faces away from earth. You can never see the far side. The moon turns itself completely around every month. The far side is kept out of your sight."

AS THE MOON SPINS AROUND WE SAY IT "ROTATES ON ITS AXIS".

“As the moon circles the earth you see more of the near side each night. You see a crescent moon first. It gets bigger until it becomes a half moon. Next it becomes a three-quarter moon. After 14 days the moon is full. For the next two weeks you see less

and less of the moon. It becomes three-quarter again, then a half moon, a crescent moon and a new moon at the end of 28 days. This happens every month.

WHEN YOU CANNOT SEE THE MOON AT ALL IT IS CALLED A "NEW MOON".

Mark and Moonbird landed. The moon has no air," said Moonbird. "That is why people cannot live here. When the astronauts came they carried special tanks filled with air so they could breathe." Mark was breathing inside the magic space bubble.

"The moon is a silent place. Sound needs air to travel. With no air there is no sound. The astronauts had to speak to each other with radios. Radio waves can travel without air," continued Moonbird.

1ST MEN ON THE MOON LANDED JULY 20TH 1969.

"With no air or water there is no weather on the moon. The moon has no snow, no clouds and no rain. Everything looks very clear," said Moonbird.

"Why do I feel so light on the moon?" asked Mark.

"Because there is less gravity on the moon than on earth," replied Moonbird. "If you weigh 60 pounds on earth you will weigh 10 pounds on the moon. You can jump farther and higher on the moon."

GRAVITY IS THE FORCE THAT PULLS US TOWARDS THE EARTH.

"You can see craters, mountains and lava seas on the moon. You can see canyons and deep valleys. The canyons are long. From far away they look like rivers, but they are dry," explained Moonbird.

"The canyons may have been formed by moon quakes, similar to earthquakes, or they may have been formed from flowing lava.

THE MOON ALSO HAS MOUNTAIN RANGES LIKE THOSE ON EARTH.

"The moon is covered in powdery dust. In places the dust is 65 feet deep. Dust is often mixed with small moon rocks. The rocks were broken into fine dust by meteorites that hit them billions of years ago."

ASTRONAUTS BROUGHT BACK MOON ROCKS TO BE STUDIED.

"An eclipse of the moon is exciting," said Moonbird as they started back to earth. "It happens when the earth comes directly between the moon and the sun. The earth blocks out the moon's light. The moon seems to disappear for several hours."

DURING AN ECLIPSE THE EARTH BLOCKS OUT THE MOON'S LIGHT.

“If earth were the size of a football, the moon would be the size of a tennisball. Because the moon is pretty big, it has a strong pull on the earth. This pull makes earth’s waters move upward. We call this rise and fall of oceans the ‘Tide’. At the beach you can see high tide and low tide. Tides are caused by the moon passing in its orbit around the earth. Land also may rise when the moon passes overhead,” Moonbird explained.

The two friends landed in Mark's room. "Men have been on the moon but have never seen a moonbird," said Mark. "They say there are no such things."
"Am I speaking to you now?" said Moonbird.
"Of course you are," said Mark.

"That's the magic about Moonbirds," said Moonbird. "We are always there if you want us to be. But people who don't believe in us will never find us." And with that, Moonbird was gone.

MOONBIRD'S MOON WORDS

SATELLITE: A SMALLER WORLD THAT CIRCLES AROUND A LARGER WORLD.

METEORITE: A METAL OR MINERAL MASS THAT HAS FALLEN ONTO THE MOON FROM OUTER SPACE.

ORBIT: THE PATH TAKEN BY THE MOON AS IT CIRCLES THE EARTH.

GRAVITY: THE FORCE THAT PULLS US TOWARD THE EARTH.

ECLIPSE: THE MOON'S LIGHT IS BLOCKED OUT BECAUSE THE EARTH COMES BETWEEN THE MOON AND THE SUN.